AUSTRALIA'S MOST
DANGEROUS
SHARKS

—

By Kathy Riley

Australian
GEOGRAPHIC

AUSTRALIA'S MOST
DANGEROUS
SHARKS

Reprinted in 2019 by

Australian GEOGRAPHIC

54 Park Street, Sydney, NSW 2000
Telephone: (02) 9163 7214
Email: editorial@ausgeo.com.au

www.australiangeographic.com.au

Australian Geographic customer service:
1300 555 176 (local call rate within Australia).
From overseas +61 2 8667 5295

Printed in China by Leo Paper Products

Funds from the sale of this book go to support the Australian Geographic Society, a not-for-profit organisation dedicated to sponsoring conservation and scientific projects, as well as adventures and expeditions.

Editor Averil Moffat
Text Kathy Riley
Book design Sue Burk
Cover design Libby De Souza
Picture research Maisie Keep & Jess Teideman
Creative director Mike Ellott
Sub-editor Amy Russell
Proofreader Ken Nina Paine
Editor-in-Chief, Australian Geographic Chrissie Goldrick
Managing Director, Australian Geographic Jo Runciman

ALSO IN THIS SERIES:

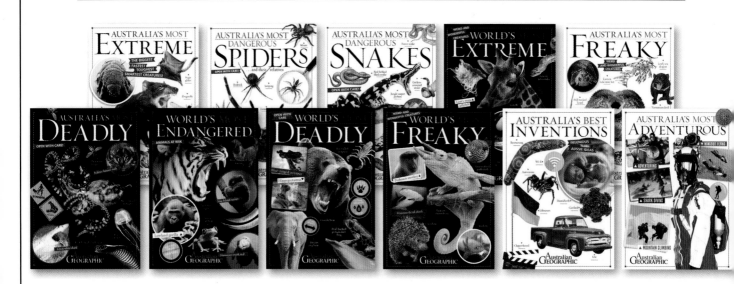

AUSTRALIA'S MOST DANGEROUS SHARKS

CONTENTS

SHARKS UP CLOSE

A shark is a type of fish. Instead of having a bony skeleton like other fish, its skeleton is made of cartilage. Cartilage is what your ears are made of. Of course, the cartilage in a shark is much thicker than your ears!

Caudal fin

Second dorsal fin

Tail

Most sharks move their tail from side to side to swim through the water. Their fins are there to help them balance.

Anal fin

Pelvic fin

FACT BOX

Sink your teeth into this!

Sharks have up to seven rows of teeth. Every time a shark loses or wears down a tooth, the one behind it moves forward to take its place. Some sharks will lose up to 35,000 teeth in a lifetime. That's a LOT of teeth!

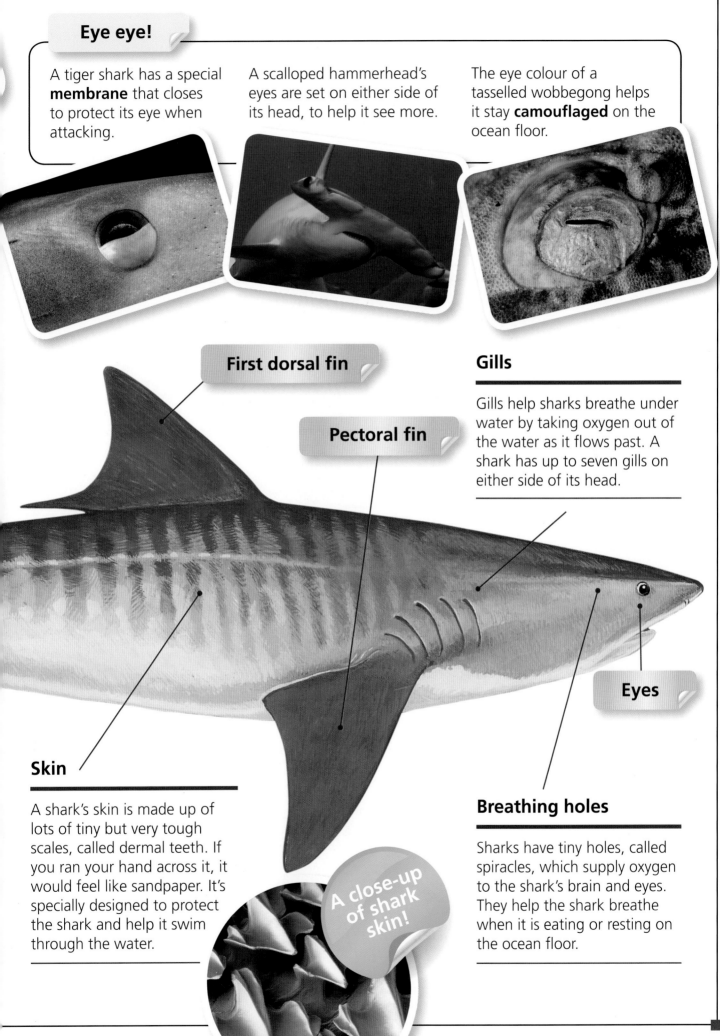

Eye eye!

A tiger shark has a special **membrane** that closes to protect its eye when attacking.

A scalloped hammerhead's eyes are set on either side of its head, to help it see more.

The eye colour of a tasselled wobbegong helps it stay **camouflaged** on the ocean floor.

First dorsal fin

Pectoral fin

Gills

Gills help sharks breathe under water by taking oxygen out of the water as it flows past. A shark has up to seven gills on either side of its head.

Eyes

Skin

A shark's skin is made up of lots of tiny but very tough scales, called dermal teeth. If you ran your hand across it, it would feel like sandpaper. It's specially designed to protect the shark and help it swim through the water.

A close-up of shark skin!

Breathing holes

Sharks have tiny holes, called spiracles, which supply oxygen to the shark's brain and eyes. They help the shark breathe when it is eating or resting on the ocean floor.

SHARKY SHAPES

There are hundreds of sharks in the world and they come in many different shapes, sizes and colours. Here are some examples.

Thresher

Up to 5.7m
Look at the long, pointy tail on this thresher shark! This tail is a mighty weapon: the shark uses it to herd small schooling fishes and then stun them so it can eat them.

Port Jackson

Up to 1.65m
This shark **forages** around the sea floor at night for starfishes, sea urchins, sea cucumbers and **molluscs**. Its blunt head and flat front teeth help it to catch and crush the hard shells of its **prey**. It also has a spine on each of its dorsal fins.

Blacktip reef

Up to 1.4m
This is a common shape among shark **species**: round in the middle, tapering to a point at each end. This design helps sharks to move through the water using as little energy as possible.

Great hammerhead

Up to 6m

This shark has a very flat, rectangular shaped head, which looks a lot like the tip of a hammer. The hammerhead shark uses its snout to pick up on tiny electrical signals **emitted** by fish and other prey, so having a bigger head helps it to hunt.

Zebra

Up to 2.35m

When it is young, this shark is stripy like a zebra. It's also known as a leopard shark, because when it gets older the stripes become spots. These spots or stripes help it to blend in with the ocean floor. Its slim body helps it to wriggle into small spaces in search of molluscs, crustaceans and fish.

Tasselled wobbegong

Up to 1.25m

The wobbegong is very wily: its mottled skin helps it to blend in with the sea floor, while the tassels around its snout look just like tasty seaweed. It lies very still until a hungry fish comes up to investigate, then it pounces!

FACT BOX

Biggest & smallest

◄ The world's smallest shark is the **pygmy shark**, which grows to only 27cm in length. That's shorter than this page.

The biggest shark ► in the world is the **whale shark**. It can grow up to 12m long. That's as long as a school bus!

GREAT WHITE SHARK

Fact File ▼

DANGER METER!

9/10 **Very dangerous**

Other names: White shark, great white, white pointer.

Length: Up to 6m.

Weight: Up to 3 tonnes. That's about the same as three cars put together!

Diet: Fish, squid, crustaceans, other sharks, sea turtles, seals, sea lions, dead or rotting animals.

Habitat: Mainly along coasts, in a wide range of water temperatures.

Breeding: A female great white shark gives birth to a live pup only once every three years. The newborn pup can be up to 1.5m long and weigh about the same as a medium-sized dog.

SHARK ALERT

The number of great white sharks in the ocean has dropped dramatically in the last 50 years. These sharks are now protected in Australian waters, which means it is illegal to harm one.

True or False?

Female great white sharks are bigger than the males.

A: True

FACT BOX — **Introducing Nicole**

Nicole is a 3.8m great white shark. In 2004 she swam from the coast of South Africa to the coast of Western Australia – a total trip of more than 11,000km – in 99 days. Six months later she was back in South Africa! Scientists were very excited, because it was the fastest long-distance ocean journey ever recorded by a marine creature. They think she might have been looking for a mate.

Did you know?

Bite-size. The jaws of a great white shark can deliver a bone-crunching bite that is more than 20 times stronger than a human's!

The teeth of a great white are the largest of any shark. This tooth is shown at actual size!

WHERE DO SHARKS LIVE?

Sharks live in oceans all over the world, and some even live in rivers and lakes. Factors affecting where sharks live include water depth, temperature and availability of food and mates.

On the move

With so much water everywhere, it's not surprising that sharks travel. Some sharks will cover many thousands of kilometres in search of food or mates. Pelagic sharks (see "Shallow or deep" box, opposite), like the great white, will roam across entire oceans. Other sharks stay close to land but still **migrate** long distances. Some sharks like to stay in the same area and not travel too far.

Tag, you're it!

In order to learn more about sharks, including where they travel, researchers will catch a shark and put a special tag on it. Then they let it go. They can then track the movement and behaviour of that shark on a computer.

A whitetip reef shark spends 98 per cent of its day resting in the same spot. As soon as the sun sets it goes hunting for food.

Did you know?

A tiger shark lives in warm tropical waters

A dogfish shark lives in cold polar waters

FACT BOX — Hot or cold?

Water temperature is a big factor in where different sharks choose to live. Many shark species prefer tropical water, where the temperature is always 21°C or higher, which is nice and warm. Tropical sharks include the tiger, whale and bull shark. A few shark species live in water that is less than 5°C, which is close to freezing. These are called polar sharks. The Greenland and dogfish shark are examples of polar sharks. Some sharks, like the great white shark, like to stay in water that is not too warm or too cold. This is called temperate water.

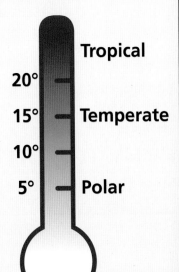

20° Tropical
15° Temperate
10°
5° Polar

FACT BOX — Shallow or deep?

Sharks that live deep in the ocean are called pelagic. The great white shark is an example of a pelagic shark. Some sharks prefer to live right on the ocean floor – they are called benthic sharks. A wobbegong is a benthic shark. Other sharks live close to the surface. The illustration below shows where some sharks live in the ocean.

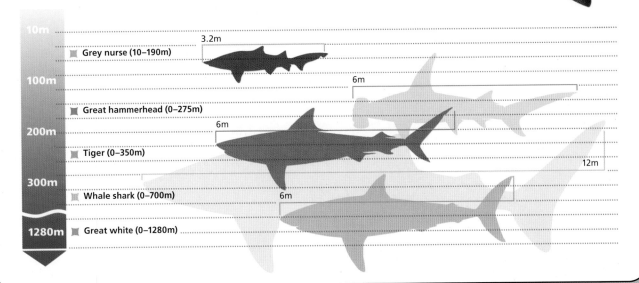

10m
100m
200m
300m
1280m

Grey nurse (10–190m) — 3.2m
Great hammerhead (0–275m) — 6m
Tiger (0–350m) — 6m
Whale shark (0–700m) — 6m
Great white (0–1280m) — 12m

GOBBLE TROUBLE

In the ocean, sharks are apex **predators**. This means there aren't any animals in the ocean that will catch and kill a shark. They are at the top of the food chain. Animals at the top of the food chain play a very important role in keeping populations of other animals in balance.

FACT BOX — **Who munches who?**

A food chain is a way of showing who eats who in a certain environment. Here are two examples of food chains in the ocean. As you can see, there is a shark at the top of both of them!

Reef sharks eat parrot fish. Parrot fish eat coral.

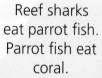

Tiger sharks eat loggerhead turtles. Loggerhead turtles eat squid. Squid eat shrimp.

What's on the menu?

All sharks are carnivorous, which means they eat other animals. Sharks eat a huge variety of animals. Fast-moving predators such as the tiger shark, bull shark and hammerhead feast on everything from fish, crustaceans and squid to sea lions, smaller sharks and seals. Some sharks even eat birds, sneaking up on them from beneath the water's surface!

Slow-moving, bottom-dwelling sharks such as the wobbegong and zebra shark eat crustaceans, molluscs and other shellfish.

Filter feeders eat tiny marine animals like krill and plankton – which is funny, because filter feeders are the largest sharks! Examples of filter feeders include whale sharks and basking sharks (below).

BASKING SHARK

Did you know?

Sharks don't drink water through their mouths. Instead, they filter sea water through their gills.

Q&A

Q: Can you fill in the blanks on this food chain?

G_____ white sharks eat _____. _____ eat octopus. Octopus eat krill. Krill eat **plankton**.

A: Great; sea lions; Sea lions

GREY NURSE SHARK

Fact File

Other names: Spotted ragged-tooth shark, sand tiger shark, blue nurse sand tiger shark.

Length: Up to 3.2m.

Age: Up to 25 years.

Diet: Fishes.

Habitat: Tropical and temperate water. It spends most of its time on the ocean floor, but also spends some time just below the water's surface.

Breeding: Grey nurse sharks give birth to two live pups about once a year.

DANGER METER!

4/10 Only dangerous if provoked

FACT BOX — Not many left

The grey nurse shark is an endangered species, which means there are not many left in the ocean, and they are at risk of being wiped out altogether. Because they don't give birth to many pups, it will take a long time for their numbers to get back to a safe level. They need our protection.

Scary teeth

Even though the grey nurse shark has rows of sharp, scary-looking teeth, it is actually quite calm and not dangerous to humans. The reason it has such sharp teeth is so it can grab and hold onto its prey.

True or False?

While they're still growing inside their mother, baby grey nurse sharks eat each other until there is only one left.

A: True

Did you know?

The grey nurse shark will poke its head out of the water and swallow air into its stomach. This helps it stay **buoyant.**

SHARK SUPERPOWERS

Sharks have been around since before dinosaurs walked the earth! It takes a very well-designed animal to survive such a long time. Sharks have developed some amazing abilities to help them become the top predators in the ocean.

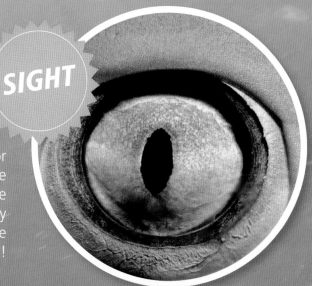

Although sharks can't see as far as they can smell or hear, they still have excellent sight in the water. Most sharks can see better in dim light than their prey. A great white, for example, swims very low in the water and searches for the outline of its prey close to the surface. By the time the prey has realised the shark is there, it's already too late!

SIGHT

VIBRATIONS

Sharks can also sense movement or vibrations in the water, using a special system of **vessels** that run underneath their skin. That's why sharks are attracted to animals – including humans and dogs – that are kicking or splashing in the water.

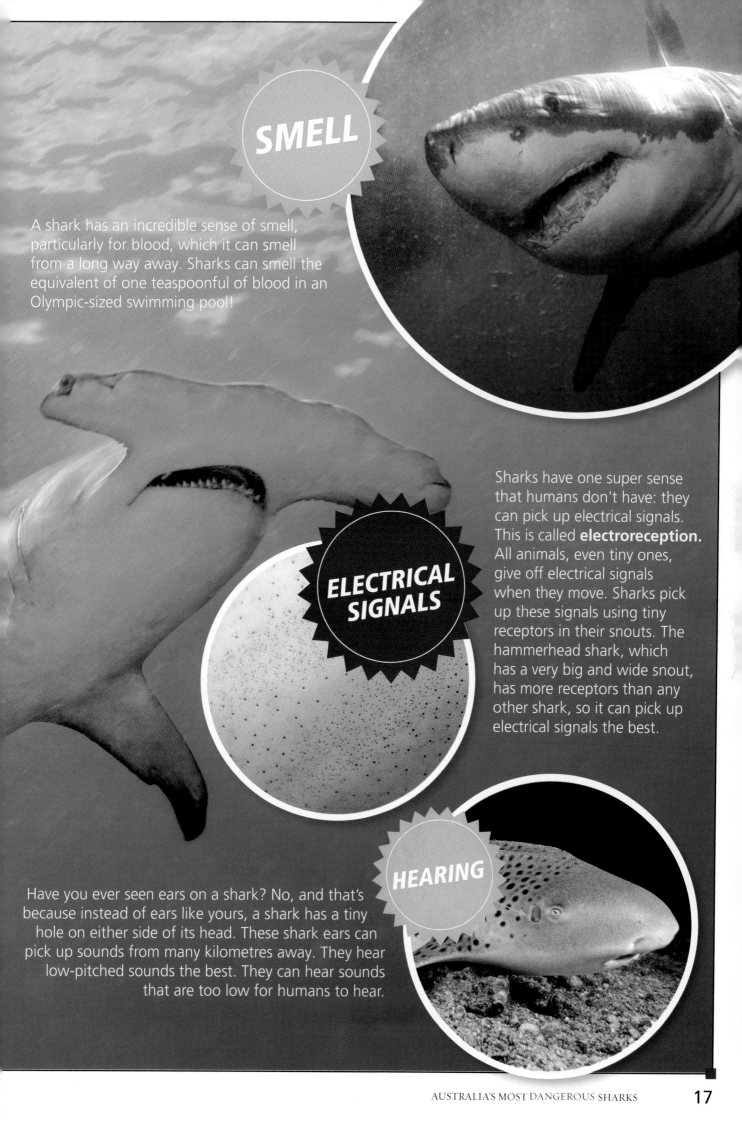

SMELL

A shark has an incredible sense of smell, particularly for blood, which it can smell from a long way away. Sharks can smell the equivalent of one teaspoonful of blood in an Olympic-sized swimming pool!

ELECTRICAL SIGNALS

Sharks have one super sense that humans don't have: they can pick up electrical signals. This is called **electroreception.** All animals, even tiny ones, give off electrical signals when they move. Sharks pick up these signals using tiny receptors in their snouts. The hammerhead shark, which has a very big and wide snout, has more receptors than any other shark, so it can pick up electrical signals the best.

HEARING

Have you ever seen ears on a shark? No, and that's because instead of ears like yours, a shark has a tiny hole on either side of its head. These shark ears can pick up sounds from many kilometres away. They hear low-pitched sounds the best. They can hear sounds that are too low for humans to hear.

TRICKS OF THE TRADE

Different sharks have developed some very useful behaviours and tricks to help them travel, hunt and feed.

Fin feet. No, sharks don't have any feet! But some sharks, such as the **whitetip reef shark** (left) or **epaulette shark**, can fold their dorsal fins over and use their pectoral fins to 'walk' forwards or backwards when hunting in small spaces.

Cookie monster. Look at the shape of this **cookie-cutter shark's** mouth. It's specially designed for feeding. First, the shark opens its mouth wide and attaches it onto the surface of its prey. Then it swivels its body around so that its teeth cut out a round, cookie-shaped piece of flesh.

Invisibility shield. The **lantern shark** has a very clever way of hiding from predators and prey. It has special organs in its skin that glow in the dark. Anything below the lantern shark thinks it is just looking at the sun shining down through the water. They can't see the shark at all!

Great white, warm blood. Most fish, including sharks, are cold-blooded. They can't control the temperature of their bodies, so they have the same body temperature as the water they are swimming in. The **great white shark**, however, can keep its body temperature steady no matter what the temperature of the water. This is why great white sharks can be such effective predators in a wide range of water temperatures.

Freshwater shark. While most sharks only live in the ocean, where the water is salty, the **bull shark** can survive in fresh water, too. This is because it can adjust its **kidneys** to suit different levels of salt in the water. Bull sharks can therefore swim up rivers, a long way from the ocean. Pretty clever!

WHALE SHARK

Did you know?

A whale shark's skin is about 15cm thick. That's about three times as thick as your wrist!

Fact File

DANGER METER!

Harmless to humans

1/10

Length: Up to 12m.

Age: Up to 100 years.

Diet: Plankton, small crustaceans and fishes, sometimes squid.

Habitat: Tropical and warm water, anywhere from the surface to very, very deep in the ocean.

Breeding: Whale sharks give birth to live young. No one has seen a whale shark give birth, and no one knows how often it happens.

Spot the difference

Each whale shark has a **unique** pattern of spots on its skin. No two whale sharks have the same pattern. This has helped scientists to identify, count and keep track of whale sharks around the world. This in turn helps us to protect these magnificent animals.

Name explained

The whale shark is a shark and NOT a whale. People call it a whale shark because it's so big, like a whale.

True or False?

Whale sharks are harmless, so it's okay to swim up and touch one.

Answer:
FALSE

Although they're harmless, whale sharks are sensitive animals and should be treated with respect. Boats and swimmers should keep a safe distance.

Big appetite for tiny fish

Even though the whale shark is the biggest fish in the ocean, it likes to eat teensy food like plankton, krill and little fish. That means it has to eat a LOT of them! It feeds by sucking huge amounts of water in through its massive mouth and out through its gills. As the water passes through, the tiny fish get caught in special filters at the back of the shark's mouth. So a whale shark is like an enormous vacuum cleaner, sucking up its dinner.

SHARK BABIES

Sharks are pretty secretive when it comes to giving birth – not many people have ever seen it happen, or even seen a newborn shark baby. This secrecy and protection is another reason why sharks are such top survivors in the ocean.

This female shark has scars from mating

FACT BOX

How do sharks breed?

Unlike bony fishes, sharks' eggs are fertilised inside the female's body. A male shark has special organs, called 'claspers', on the underside of his body, which he uses to latch on to the female to fertilise her eggs. During mating, the male often bites the female on her back and fins to help him get into the right position.

Most sharks give birth to live young, but some sharks – like the Port Jackson shark – lay eggs, which are left among seaweed or wedged into rocks.

When the baby shark is born, it already has a full set of teeth! Most sharks are born ready to swim away and start hunting. They don't need their parents to look after them.

The number of babies born depends on the type of shark. Some species only give birth to one or two babies. Others can give birth to up to 100 babies at a time.

The amount of time the baby takes to develop inside the mother (known as the gestation period) also depends on the species. The **gestation** period for sharks ranges from about nine months (which is the same as a human baby) to as long as two years.

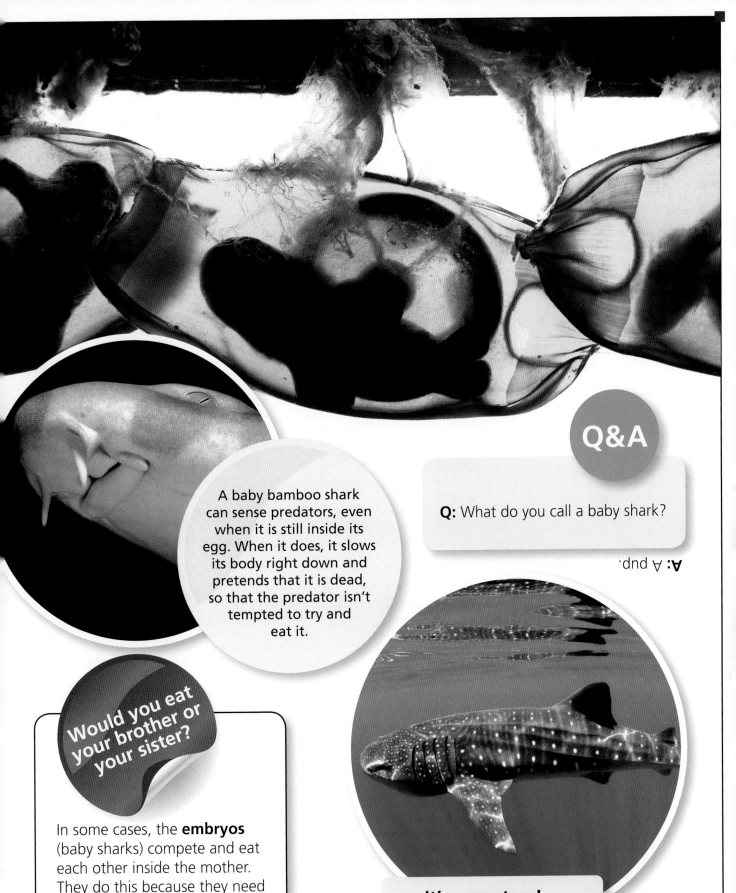

A baby bamboo shark can sense predators, even when it is still inside its egg. When it does, it slows its body right down and pretends that it is dead, so that the predator isn't tempted to try and eat it.

Q&A

Q: What do you call a baby shark?

A: A pup.

Would you eat your brother or your sister?

In some cases, the **embryos** (baby sharks) compete and eat each other inside the mother. They do this because they need nourishment to help them survive and grow, so their natural instinct is to eat their brothers or sisters – for food and to ensure their own survival.

It's a mystery!

Nobody has ever seen whale sharks mate or give birth. In fact, no one really knows how many babies a whale shark can give birth to. Only one pregnant whale shark has ever been seen.

SHARK SCHOOL

Dive into this page full of wonderful shark facts!

Turning a shark upside down stops it from moving.

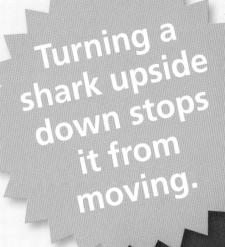

You can tell a shark's length by the size of its teeth

Great white vs Megalodon

Megalodon is the great white shark's ancestor. Its teeth measured up to 21cm (a great white shark's grow up to 5cm) and suggest the animal reached about 16m in length.

Lots of sharks are pale underneath and darker on top. This is called **countershading,** and it helps them hunt. If they're above their prey, they blend in with the light from the sky, and if they're below, they can hide in the shadows.

Bee stings kill more people than great white sharks each year.

The spiny dogfish shark has the longest known lifespan of any shark – it can live for more than 100 years!

Q&A

Q: What do you call a gathering of sharks?

A: A shiver.

Although a bony fish has a gas-filled swim bladder to stop it sinking, a shark has a huge, oily liver. The oil in the liver is lighter than the water, so it gives the shark some buoyancy. However, the shark is still a lot heavier than the water, so it has to keep swimming to stay afloat.

WOBBEGONG

Fact File ▼

Other names: Carpet shark.

Length: Up to 3m.

Weight: Up to 70kg.

Diet: Small fishes, crabs, crayfish and octopuses.

Habitat: Shallow water around the coast of Australia. They spend most of their time on the seabed.

Breeding: Wobbegongs breed only once every three years. They give birth to large numbers of live pups.

DANGER METER!

3/10 Harmless unless provoked

SNEAKY

The wobbegong is an ambush predator. This means that instead of actively hunting its prey, the wobbegong lies still on the ocean floor and waits for prey to approach. When the time is right, it lunges with lightning-fast reflexes and snags the fish in its sharp teeth.

Fish, chips and leather

Although wobbegongs don't eat humans, humans eat wobbegongs! Wobbegong meat is popular in fish and chips shops. Their skin is also used to make leather.

Did you know?

The word wobbegong is thought to come from an Aboriginal word meaning 'shaggy beard', which describes the tassels around the shark's mouth.

True or False?

If you grab a wobbegong by the tail it can't bite you.

Answer: FALSE

These sharks are very flexible, and could easily swing around and catch your hand. Better leave it alone!

FACT BOX   How many wobbegongs?

There are 10 different species of wobbegong. Most of them are found in Australian waters.

WEIRD AND WONDERFUL

A selection of some of the most unusual sharks from around the world.

▶ Basking shark

This is the second-largest living shark, next to the whale shark. Like the whale shark, it feeds on tiny fish by sucking water in through its mouth, catching the fish in filters at the back of its mouth, then pushing the water back out through its gills. Its big nose has led to one of its other names: the elephant shark.

▶ Angel shark

This shark looks more like a ray than a shark. It has a really flat body and large pectoral fins. The colour of its skin allows it to blend in with the ocean floor and hide from its prey. When something tasty comes close, it suddenly bursts forward and quickly snaps it up.

Goblin shark

With an extremely long snout, long jaws and pink body, the goblin shark is one very strange-looking shark! It lives in the very deep parts of the ocean, where there's no sunlight. That means it can't see its prey – instead, it picks up on their electrical signals. When it gets close, it sucks its prey in close to its mouth and then gobbles it!

Sawshark

No prizes for guessing where this shark got its name from! The sawshark's nose is like a big saw, with teeth running along the edges. It cruises along the sea floor, and when it finds its prey, it swings its nose from side to side, which whacks and cripples its prey.

Frilled shark

This shark looks like a cross between a snake, an eel and a lizard. It grows to about 2m, or as long as a bicycle. It is a very rare shark that usually swims in the deep ocean. It has big gill slits, which look like frills around its neck. It also has lots and lots of sharp teeth, which it uses to bite into squid and small fish.

WHO'S SCARIER: THEM OR US?

It's true that sharks can sometimes attack humans, causing serious injury or even death. But there are also lots of ways that humans can injure or kill sharks. In many ways, sharks have more to fear from us than we do from them.

FACT BOX — Threats to sharks

Fishing

Large numbers of sharks are caught each year. Individual fishers like the challenge of catching a shark, while big fishing companies, called fisheries, catch sharks to sell. A fisher may often kill a shark without knowing it. Lots of sharks will get away when they bite and swallow the hook. The hook gets caught inside them, which makes them get sick and die.

Bycatch

Another big cause of shark deaths is when they are caught accidentally by fisheries who are targeting another species. This is called **bycatch.**

Shark nets

Shark nets are nets that are put up just off the coast of swimming beaches in Australia, to stop sharks from entering and attacking swimmers. Unfortunately, sharks sometimes get tangled up in these nets and drown.

Shark finning

The majority of sharks killed each year are killed for their fins. Shark fin soup is a popular dish in some countries and people pay a lot of money for it. The sharks are often caught, finned, and then thrown back into the ocean to slowly die, so shark finning is very cruel as well as destructive.

More than 100 million sharks worldwide are killed by humans each year. That is a LOT of sharks. Shark populations are dropping very quickly, and some shark species are in danger of disappearing altogether.

Big bite!

Rodney Fox is lucky to have survived when a great white shark attacked him off the coast of South Australia in 1963. He needed 465 stitches. Far from being afraid of sharks, Rodney has since fought hard for their protection.

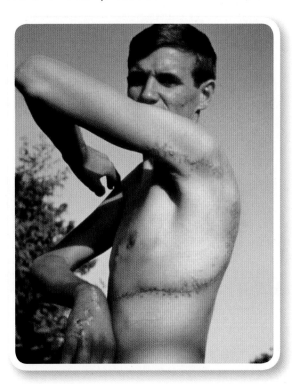

FACT BOX

Steer clear of sharks

Here are five tips for shark-safe swimming:

1. Swim at beaches that are patrolled by surf lifesavers.

2. Do not swim in areas known for dangerous sharks.

3. Avoid swimming or surfing alone.

4. Avoid swimming or surfing at dawn, dusk or night. These are typically the feeding times for a lot of sharks.

5. Check deep water carefully before jumping in from a boat.

Shark-safe tips

Glossary

buoyant	Able to float or rise in water.
bycatch	When trawlers' nets catch some kinds of fish accidentally.
camouflage	The way an animal or plant disguises itself by looking like it is part of its surroundings.
countershading	Special light and dark areas on animals that help hide or protect them.
electroreception	The ability to detect electrical signals.
embryo	An unborn creature.
emit	Give out or send out.
forage	Look for food.
gestation	Time it takes for a baby to develop inside its mother.
habitat	The type of environment an animal lives in.
kidney	A filtering organ in the body.
membrane	A very thin layer.
migration	Travel from one place to another.
mollusc	An invertebrate animal with a shell.
plankton	Very tiny plants and animals that live and float in the water.
predator	An animal that hunts and eats other animals.
prey	An animal that is hunted by other animals.
species	A group of animals that are basically the same.
unique	Unlike any other.
vessel	A tube in the body that carries blood or another fluid.

FURTHER READING

Scary Sharks
Camilla de la Bedoyere, 2012, QED

Investigate Sharks
Greg Pyers, 2000, Whitecap Books

Sharks
Reader's Digest editors, 1998, Reader's Digest

Sharks
Erik D. Stoops and Sherrie Stoops, 1994, Sterling Publishing

PHOTOGRAPHER AND ILLUSTRATOR CREDITS
Page numbers are followed by image position indicated clockwise from top left of page.

Kelvin Aitken 4 (3); Justin Bailie/Getty 30 (2); Franco Banfi/Getty 10 (3), 21 (2), 26 (3); Gary Bell/Oceanwide Images 4 (1), 7 (3), 16 (1,3), 22 (4); Jonathan Bird/Getty 24 (1), 27 (1); David Bristow 29 (1); Antonio Busiello/Getty 13 (1); Mark Conlin/Getty 17 (2), 19 (2); Corbis 5 (3); Marje Crosby-Fairall Cover (1,4,5,6,7), title page (2,4), 4 (2), 6 (1,2,3,4), 7 (1,2), 11 (3), 14 (2), 26 (2), back cover (2,3,4,6); Bill Curtsinger/Getty 18 (4); Susan Dabritz/Seapics.com 28 (1); Ethan Daniels/Getty 26 (1); Chuck Davis/Getty title page (1), 8 (1); Karen Doody/Stocktrek/Getty 15 (2), 23 (3); Hauke Dressler/Getty 31 (3); Antoni Emchowitz/Getty 9 (1); David Fleetham/Oceanwide Images 12 (3), 17 (3), 23 (1); Stephen Frink/Getty 12 (5), 17 (1); Getty 5 (4), 11 (1,2); Armando F. Jenik/Getty 12 (1); Paul Kay/Getty 30 (1); Dorling Kindersley/Getty cover (3b), title page (3b), 18 (3), 32 (1b), back cover (1); Rudie Kuiter/Oceanwide Images 28 (4); Sharon Lapkin/Getty 25 (2); Albert Lleal/Getty 18 (2); Wayne Lynch/Getty 25 (1); Frederick R. McConnaughey/Getty 18 (1); Mike McCoy 12 (4,7); Andy Murch/Oceanwide Images 25 (3,4), 28 (2); Oxford Scientific Films/Getty 13 (3); Doug Perrine/Seapics.com cover (3a), title page (3a), 9 (2), 22 (2); Photo Researchers/Getty 22 (1,3); Peter Pinnock/Getty 12 (2), 14 (1); Jeffrey L. Rotman/Getty 5 (1), 15 (1), 16 (2), 21 (1), 23 (2), 24 (2), 30 (3), 31 (1,2); Alexander Safonov/Getty 19 (1); Luis Javier Sandoval/Getty 5 (2); Denis Scott/Corbis 9 (3); Mike Severns/Getty 12 (6); Brian J. Skerry/Getty 13 (2); Kevin Stead cover (2), 8 (2), 20 (2), back cover (5); Oliver Strewe/Getty 31 (4); Ron and Valerie Taylor 3 (1,2), 10 (1,2,4); David Tipling/Getty 32 (1a); Steven Trainoff/Getty 20 (1); Masa Ushioda/Seapics.com 7 (4).